Spring, Too, Returns

Spring, Too, Returns

CHRISTINE TRAN

RESOURCE *Publications* · Eugene, Oregon

SPRING, TOO, RETURNS

Resource Publications
An Imprint of Wipf and Stock Publishers
199 W. 8th Ave., Suite 3
Eugene, OR 97401

www.wipfandstock.com

PAPERBACK ISBN: 978-1-6667-5355-4
HARDCOVER ISBN: 978-1-6667-5356-1
EBOOK ISBN: 978-1-6667-5357-8

AUGUST 16, 2022 4:16 PM

Dedicated to the ones who brought spring to my heart.

Contents

Winter Rude

Winter may be rude,
And her winds may be crude,
But as her days prolong,
You realize that you too, can be strong.
She teaches you to persevere,
And to stay nowhere but here.
In the midst of her every storm,
Your Strength will ever keep you warm.

Winter True

To herself, winter remains true,
Even as your comfort runs dry and through.
She puts your perseverance to the test;
As all the world lays at rest.
She whispers to keep pressing on,
And pass through the darkness of dawn.
The shadows cannot subdue the skies,
As the light comes from the sunrise.

Winter Cold

The winter cold matches that of my heart,
Now that we have grown apart.
No love to treasure,
No romance to measure.
Heart wounded like a bruised reed,
No warmth and care that I need.
Is it better to be alone,
Than to have a wintry heart of stone?

Winter Brutal

Winter brings the brutal truth,
Just like the passing of one's youth.
Her cruelty you can withstand,
Though her outbreaks cannot be planned.
As you walk through the wintry cold,
You admire the pioneers of old.
Think of the heroes of the past—
Be brave and hold steadfast.

Winter Tempest

Our love became the tempest fury,
So, she had to leave in a hurry.
One moment hot, another cold,
He was no longer there to uphold.
Even the winter storm could be subdued,
But could love lost be renewed?
Rather than to maim or destroy,
Love is meant for bliss and joy.

Winter Blue

Without him, it is a winter blue.
Yet, it is better that we are through.
She could not handle the degradation—
Love undone is rather a desecration.
Can't we go back to that July?
Love was aglow without tears to cry.
Now, all she knows is winter's cold.
Everything feels recycled and old.

Winter's Fallow

Sometimes fallow is what we need,
Abundance can produce greed.
Should the winter tree not blossom,
My gratitude should still be wholesome.
A time to reap, a time to sow;
A time to stay, a time to go.
Winter reminds one to rest;
Not every season is meant for harvest.

Winter Sleep

Winter is when all the world is asleep,
Untroubled in a slumber so deep.
How will you taste the warmth sweet,
Unless the bitter cold you did meet?
There is value found in opposition,
Such as the sun and her varied positions.
How can we treasure day without night?
Darkness makes known the glory of light.

Winter's Warmth

When all we hear is the wind's howl,
And all around us feels rather foul.
Love will keep us safe and warm,
And brave every cowardly storm.
At your voice, the rain will hush,
As my cheeks retain their first blush.
No matter the fury we face,
Love is our saving grace.

Winter Snow

Though my sins are scarlet red aglow,
I can be made as white as winter snow.
None of us can claim perfection;
That is the power of love and affection.
Forgive, so you can be forgiven;
Such is the word from Heaven.
All of us can be made new and redeemed,
No matter how far off we seemed.

Christmas Hope

Christmas represents hope and anticipation,
As gifts flood the whole nation.
'Tis better to give than to receive;
At least, that's what givers believe.
It's not simply about material things,
But the joy that an act of kindness brings.
Spreading love can last a lifetime,
And does not cost one a single dime.

New Year

What is your hope for the new year?
To be steadfast and not shed another tear?
There is strength also in fragility,
Do not be ashamed of your vulnerability.
You are the unique, incredible you.
Through adversity, you held on and grew.
No one gets to dictate your journey;
There is no rush or hurry.

Winter's Wait

Winter is when we silently wait—
Though as humans, that's what we hate.
We long for better things to come,
Though all around us is glum.
All around us is buried beneath the snow,
While we long for the spring glow.
They say that hope springs eternal within us,
Even if we are dust to dust.

Winter's Adieu

Just when we were bidding winter adieu,
A wintry storm comes through.
What is life without a little surprise,
Lest we profess to be too wise.
When the road deviates from expectation,
We can soar without limitation.
If we learn to keep an open heart and mind,
A surprise can be a gift of an unexpected kind.

Winter's Undoing

With just a touch, winter is undone,
And before your eyes, spring has begun.
It teaches us the beauty of waiting,
And haste is worth forsaking.
Certain people may be seasonal,
But true love is eternal.
May you find what you are searching for—
That love is waiting at your door.

Spring, Too, Returns

Spring, too, returns after a long wait.
Her renewal for you is at the gate.
No matter how brutal winter has been,
Spring promises you can start afresh again.
Look at the green bud that blooms anew,
No matter the fallow that it grows through.
Catch your breath and find your calm,
Look to the morning and release every qualm.

Spring's Strength

Spring simply cannot be subdued,
No matter if the winter is long or rude.
She waits with her quiet strength,
As winter insists upon its length.
When winter overstays his welcome,
We grow ever more crestfallen.
Until we see the green bud on the tree,
We're reminded that we, too, can be free.

Jasmine

Look to the jasmine bloom,
And take in her sweet perfume.
Even when she seems barren,
She reminds you to wait for the season.
Even as her flower withers to the ground,
The beauty of her greenery can be found.
While it is agonizing to sit and wait,
Much patience and endurance it will create.

Magnolia

The magnolia tree is a late and transient bloom;
Despite its beauty, it fades too soon.
Once flowers of brilliant pink and red,
It turns brown and begins to shed.
How could beauty turn into decay?
I suppose our love story also happened that way.
The seasonality to life we must accept,
And the treasured memories should be well-kept.

Rose

Why is the rose the epitome of love?
Is her beauty sent from above?
We have cheapened love by the dozen,
By our romance, we are brazen.
Love cannot be commercialized,
But rather through actions realized.
Let us do none for selfish gain,
But be selfless through joy and pain.

Olive Shoots

Your offspring will be like the olive shoots,
Plentiful like the harvest fruits.
You will pass down your wisdom and joy;
Your lessons, they will employ.
You will learn sacrificial love;
The greatest gift from above.
You will build a legacy that will last—
That you can look forward beyond the past.

Harvest

After a season of fallow and rest,
Comes abundance and harvest.
You will reap what you invest and sow,
Under the sun's impartial and universal glow,
Even the ones more shriveled than you've seen,
Can recover to become lush and green.
May your garden come alive,
That you may bloom and thrive.

Springtime & Resurrection

No matter how many times she dies,
Just like the phoenix, she rises.
Springtime is the season of resurrection;
When all is reborn as a new creation.
Breathe in that fresh spring air,
For the first time, dream, if you dare.
Open your eyes and take in the light,
Expand your wings and let them take flight.

Springtime Doubt

The spring bud can sometimes doubt,
Whether she can bloom and sprout.
After a vicious winter,
She is often left feeling bitter.
All doubts do is betray,
So we should chase them away.
Those who hope always win,
For the sun still rises again.

Springtime Pruning

Nothing is as torturous as a pruning,
But just as an instrument, you need fine tuning.
Cutting certain branches bears more fruit,
As you, the Gardener, grow more astute.
The withering branch must be sacrificed,
For the greater good of the tree, that is the price.
Once the pain of the pruning has passed,
Comes the beauty of harvest that will surely last.

Renewal

Even if you feel dry like a carcass,
And the cracks rupture on the surface,
Springtime is about renewal,
No matter how life has been cruel.
Listen to the morning sparrow's cry,
Look at how she is nimble and spry.
Look to the spring bud, green and hopeful—
Reminding us that rebirth is eternal.

Barren

Even as you feel barren and dry,
Endless are the tears that you cry.
Remain steadfast as you wait,
There is a harvest in your fate.
Comparison is a taunter and a liar;
Look not to the table of your neighbor.
As you strive and fear less,
You will see you are greatly blessed.

Green Pasture

I want to walk by the green pasture,
And know that my peace is sure.
When all within me is still,
Even my strong will.
I am steady and unperturbed,
That life cannot leave me disturbed.
All I feel is the calm breeze;
All within me is at ease.

Wait

Springtime teaches me to patiently wait;
No matter how unknown is my fate.
I have to trust the best is yet to come;
So, I do not grow weary and glum.
While the road is long and weathered,
To hope I must stay tethered.
Waiting keeps me virtuous,
And enables me to grow courageous.

February

February brought me into existence;
Whether it is spring or winter is met with resistance.
In a month where love is celebrated,
You can be sure that many despise it.
One day can feel like balmy summer,
While the next feels like winter bitter.
When life can be unpredictable,
Perhaps that is why it is so wonderful.

April 30th

My mother was always told her birth was a dark day,
As the fall of Saigon twisted it that way.
Every birth should be deemed a miraculous thing,
Consider the joy it does bring.
Every human is of importance and worth,
And that begins with their first breath on Earth.
If they try to disparage and devalue you,
You must hold those lies to be untrue.

At Long Last

At long last, summer is here.
We wish you would not soon disappear.
After the cruelty of winter and spring,
We have longed for the warmth you bring.
You are like a lover that soon leaves,
Left in the aftermath of you, she grieves.
Summer is meant to be enjoyed for the moment.
Your brevity, she will lament.

Lemonade

Lemonade will always remind me of you;
It was always the drink you'd come to.
It is the epitome of warm summer days,
Even if it meant spending it in a laze.
Its coldness is perfect for the heat;
There is no taste quite as sweet.
I will drink one in your memory,
As you exist only in my reverie.

Summer Nights

Summer nights are about that cool breeze,
And make your heart feel at ease.
Sitting under the moonlight,
I wish we could take flight.
As the wind tousles through your hair,
You surrender your worries without a care,
Summer eases your every senseless doubt,
That you can be free to be out and about.

Sun Shower

Have you ever seen a sun shower—
When the sun and rain coexist in power?
Life can be strange and wonderful,
When its paradoxes are bountiful.
We don't always know what to expect,
What beauty can be found in the imperfect.
Look for the sunshine in your rain,
What surprises you can ease your pain.

Lavender Fields

I am dreaming of lavender fields,
And the fragrance it yields.
It will transport you to France,
And make you think of romance.
When you need a restful sleep,
It will draw you into a slumber deep.
Leave your worries at the door,
And take in its sweetness once more.

Summer Sun

The radiance the summer sun
Cannot be avoided by anyone.
From afar, she rules with an iron fist,
And we humans cannot resist.
In the midst of the winter storm,
All we long for is to be warm.
Yet with a fierceness she comes,
All we want to do is run.

Summer Dew

Look at the freshness of the summer dew,
It reminds us that all can be made new.
To the blades of grass it clings,
New life it does promise to bring.
Take in that crisp summer air,
Your worries will dissipate without a care.
May then your soul find rest,
The seasons always know best.

June

Summer always begins in June,
It never comes a moment too soon.
Like children, we wait with anticipation,
And cannot be taken with sleep or sedation.
We long to be by the lake or oceanside,
As the waves follow the moon's tide.
If only summer never did end,
Under the sun all our days we would spend.

July

You came to me at July's end,
And I wondered if you were a God-send.
You held me with arms so strong,
Suddenly, I felt I could belong.
My skin was dewy and sun-kissed;
This was the romance I had missed.
Now that you are gone,
I still think of you at the summer dawn.

August

Do not weep when summer departs,
Yet remember how it warms our hearts.
Ponder upon the salmon sky,
Meditate on the hummingbird's cry.
Summer will go, and yet it will return,
With each year, how much more you will learn.
Gently let go and bid adieu;
Life is cyclical and never quite through.

Autumn Breeze

When summer has overstayed her welcome,
Oh, how we long for autumn.
The changing color of the trees,
And that sweet, easy breeze.
While summer is for fast living,
Autumn is far more forgiving.
Look at the foliage and slow down your pace,
As the evening sun kisses your face.

September Goodbye

We bid goodbye that September,
But your memory, I will ever remember.
Fall is on the horizon,
And farewell is the road we've chosen.
It will be a cold autumn without you,
Since we have said adieu.
I have to love myself,
And treasure self-worth above all else.

September Blue

I enter a state of September blue,
Whenever I ponder and think of you.
When on that fated day, you left,
And upon my heart you committed theft.
All around the world is changing season,
You gave up the fight without reason.
Love is worth it, so I am told—
But I would rather have peace as I grow old.

Wither

All my plants are starting to wither,
As they know, after autumn comes winter.
A time to grow and a time to rest,
Expectation knows what's best.
Life is not always lush and green;
A bloom cannot always be seen.
Even if the season is barren and dry,
Hold onto hope you must try.

Thanksgiving

Thanksgiving reminds us to be full of gratitude,
It's the only way we can reach the highest altitude.
There is always reason to be thankful,
We must awaken our hearts from the lull.
Even when we are filled with much doubt,
When we give thanks, the garden still does sprout.
Find purpose in your life to be grateful for,
And all the beauty that lies in store.

Yellow

The yellow of the fall leaves is bright,
Shining and reflecting the sunlight.
The brilliance overcomes the dark,
Just with one solitary light spark.
When all around is filled with color,
We cannot help but be filled with wonder.
Perhaps to savor and protect the Earth's beauty
Is part of our citizens' duty.

Red

When the leaves turn a bright blood red,
We're reminded we are alive and not dead.
Red is the color of vigor and passion,
That we are formed in the highest fashion.
Just like the blood that courses through our veins,
The seasons endure through the snow and rain.
When the foliage shines with much brilliance,
We are inspired to have strength and resilience.

Gratitude

Gratitude is a posture of the heart,
An attitude you practice as a fine art.
It is constant, rather than circumstantial,
Its fruits are always substantial.
If you hold fast onto gratefulness,
You will reap its benefits.
In darkness, you will always see the light,
You will never again fear the night.

Change

No matter how the seasons are changed,
In much beauty they are arranged.
Perhaps, I, too, can grow,
And have much fruition to show.
Whenever I feel afraid,
I see that the flowers are wonderfully arrayed.
When all around me is in bloom,
I will no longer feel gloom.